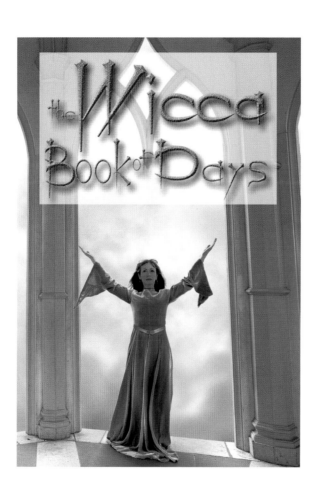

The Wicca Book of Days

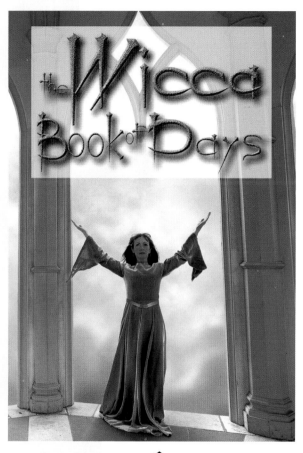

Sheena Morgan

vega

Author's acknowledgements

Its difficult to know where to begin in thanking people for their efforts because everyone involved worked so hard.

Thanks first to Jane Alexander for the best kind of advice and for going without sleep for 48 hours in Cornwall so we could get everything done. To David and Indi for putting up with having their home regularly transformed into a floral crown factory. To Mark Buckingham for his enthusiasm and technical magic and to Neil Sutherland for his unfailing optimism and willingness to clamber about in the wilds from dawn to dusk, just to get the right shot. Thanks too to Michelle, Michael and Inbaal for being such fantastic models. And finally, special thanks to Mike and Agni, for bravery beyond the call of duty. Only we will know just how frosty it was at dawn on that December morning or how wet and freezing a long barrow can be. Thank you again for all your hard work.

If you would like to find out more about Wicca, you can contact me by sending an SAE to:

Rowan Tree and Red Thread
PO Box 11
Rye
TN31 6WP

© Vega 2002
Text © Sheena Morgan

ISBN 1-84333-622-7

A catalogue record for this book is available from the British Library

First published in 2002 by
Vega
64 Brewery Road
London, N7 9NT

A member of **Chrysalis** Books plc

Visit our website at
www.chrysalisbooks.co.uk

Printed and bound in China

Design, illustration and retouching:
Mark Buckingham
Project management: Jane Alexander
Photography: Neil Sutherland, Steve Morley
Production: Susan Sutterby

The publishers would also like to thank Robert Kennedy of the Wand Workshop (info@wandworkshop.co.uk) for the kind loan of his crystal wands and Ninya Mikhaila, Penny Murphy and Sarah Davies for their generous assistance.

Contents

Moon Charts

2003

Jan

Mon	Tues	Wed	Thur	Fri	Sat	Sun
		1	2●	3	4	5
6	7	8	9	10☽	11	12
13	14	15	16	17	18○	19
20	21	22	23	24	25☾	26
27	28	29	30	31		

Feb

Mon	Tues	Wed	Thur	Fri	Sat	Sun
					1●	2
3	4	5	6	7	8	9☽
10	11	12	13	14	15	16○
17	18	19	20	21	22	23☾
24	25	26	27	28		

Mar

Mon	Tues	Wed	Thur	Fri	Sat	Sun
					1	2
3●	4	5	6	7	8	9
10	11☽	12	13	14	15	16
17	18○	19	20	21	22	23
24	25☾	26	27	28	29	30
31						

Apr

Mon	Tues	Wed	Thur	Fri	Sat	Sun
	1●	2	3	4	5	6
7	8	9☽	10	11	12	13
14	15	16○	17	18	19	20
21	22	23☾	24	25	26	27
28	29	30				

May

Mon	Tues	Wed	Thur	Fri	Sat	Sun
			1●	2	3	4
5	6	7	8	9☽	10	11
12	13	14	15	16○	17	18
19	20	21	22	23☾	24	25
26	27	28	29	30	31●	

June

Mon	Tues	Wed	Thur	Fri	Sat	Sun
						1
2	3	4	5	6	7☽	8
9	10	11	12	13	14○	15
16	17	18	19	20	21☾	22
23	24	25	26	27	28	29●
30						

July

Mon	Tues	Wed	Thur	Fri	Sat	Sun
	1	2	3	4	5	6
7☽	8	9	10	11	12	13○
14	15	16	17	18	19	20
21☾	22	23	24	25	26	27
28	29●	30	31			

Aug

Mon	Tues	Wed	Thur	Fri	Sat	Sun
				1	2	3
4	5☽	6	7	8	9	10
11	12	13	14○	15	16	17
18	19	20☾	21	22	23	24
25	26	27●	28	29	30	31

Sept

Mon	Tues	Wed	Thur	Fri	Sat	Sun
1	2	3☽	4	5	6	7
8	9	10○	11	12	13	14
15	16	17	18☾	19	20	21
22	23	24	25	26●	27	28
29	30					

Oct

Mon	Tues	Wed	Thur	Fri	Sat	Sun
		1	2☽	3	4	5
6	7	8	9	10○	11	12
13	14	15	16	17	18☾	19
20	21	22	23	24	25●	26
27	28	29	30	31		

Nov

Mon	Tues	Wed	Thur	Fri	Sat	Sun
					1☽	2
3	4	5	6	7	8	9○
10	11	12	13	14	15	16
17☾	18	19	20	21	22	23●
24	25	26	27	28	29	30☽

Dec

Mon	Tues	Wed	Thur	Fri	Sat	Sun
1	2	3	4	5	6	7
8●	9	10	11	12	13	14
15	16☾	17	18	19	20	21
22	23●	24	25	26	27	28
29	30☽	31				
Mon	Tues	Wed	Thur	Fri	Sat	Sun

2004

Jan

Mon	Tues	Wed	Thur	Fri	Sat	Sun
			1	2	3	4
5	6	7○	8	9	10	11
12	13	14	15☾	16	17	18
19	20	21●	22	23	24	25
26	27	28	29☽	30	31	

Feb

Mon	Tues	Wed	Thur	Fri	Sat	Sun
						1
2	3	4	5	6○	7	8
9	10	11	12	13☾	14	15
16	17	18	19	20●	21	22
23	24	25	26	27	28☽	29

Mar

Mon	Tues	Wed	Thur	Fri	Sat	Sun
1	2	3	4	5	6○	7
8	9	10	11	12	13☾	14
15	16	17	18	19	20●	21
22	23	24	25	26	27	28☽
29	30	31				

Apr

Mon	Tues	Wed	Thur	Fri	Sat	Sun
			1	2	3	4
5○	6	7	8	9	10	11
12☾	13	14	15	16	17	18
19●	20	21	22	23	24	25
26	27☽	28	29	30		

May

Mon	Tues	Wed	Thur	Fri	Sat	Sun
					1	2
3	4○	5	6	7	8	9
10	11☾	12	13	14	15	16
17	18	19●	20	21	22	23
24	25	26	27☽	28	29	30
31						

June

Mon	Tues	Wed	Thur	Fri	Sat	Sun
	1	2	3○	4	5	6
7	8	9☾	10	11	12	13
14	15	16	17●	18	19	20
21	22	23	24	25☽	26	27
28	29	30				

July

Mon	Tues	Wed	Thur	Fri	Sat	Sun
			1	2○	3	4
5	6	7	8	9☾	10	11
12	13	14	15	16	17●	18
19	20	21	22	23	24	25☽
26	27	28	29	30	31○	

Aug

Mon	Tues	Wed	Thur	Fri	Sat	Sun
						1
2	3	4	5	6	7☾	8
9	10	11	12	13	14	15
16●	17	18	19	20	21	22
23☽	24	25	26	27	28	29
30○	31					

Sept

Mon	Tues	Wed	Thur	Fri	Sat	Sun
		1	2	3	4	5
6☾	7	8	9	10	11	12
13	14●	15	16	17	18	19
20	21☽	22	23	24	25	26
27	28○	29	30			

Oct

Mon	Tues	Wed	Thur	Fri	Sat	Sun
				1	2	3
4	5	6☾	7	8	9	10
11	12	13	14●	15	16	17
18	19	20☽	21	22	23	24
25	26	27	28○	29	30	31

Nov

Mon	Tues	Wed	Thur	Fri	Sat	Sun
1	2	3	4	5☾	6	7
8	9	10	11	12●	13	14
15	16	17	18	19☽	20	21
22	23	24	25	26○	27	28
29	30					

Dec

Mon	Tues	Wed	Thur	Fri	Sat	Sun
		1	2	3	4	5☾
6	7	8	9	10	11	12●
13	14	15	16	17	18☽	19
20	21	22	23	24	25	26○
27	28	29	30	31		
Mon	Tues	Wed	Thur	Fri	Sat	Sun

2005

Jan
Mon	Tues	Wed	Thur	Fri	Sat	Sun
					1	2
3☾	4	5	6	7	8	9
10●	11	12	13	14	15	16
17☽	18	19	20	21	22	23
24	25○	26	27	28	29	30
31						

Feb
Mon	Tues	Wed	Thur	Fri	Sat	Sun
	1	2☾	3	4	5	6
7	8●	9	10	11	12	13
14	15	16☽	17	18	19	20
21	22	23	24○	25	26	27
28						

Mar
Mon	Tues	Wed	Thur	Fri	Sat	Sun
	1	2	3☾	4	5	6
7	8	9	10●	11	12	13
14	15	16	17☽	18	19	20
21	22	23	24	25○	26	27
28	29	30	31			

Apr
Mon	Tues	Wed	Thur	Fri	Sat	Sun
				1	2☾	3
4	5	6	7	8●	9	10
11	12	13	14	15	16☽	17
18	19	20	21	22	23	24○
25	26	27	28	29	30	

May
Mon	Tues	Wed	Thur	Fri	Sat	Sun
						1☾
2	3	4	5	6	7	8●
9	10	11	12	13	14	15
16☽	17	18	19	20	21	22
23○	24	25	26	27	28	29
30☾	31					

June
Mon	Tues	Wed	Thur	Fri	Sat	Sun
		1	2	3	4	5
6●	7	8	9	10	11	12
13	14	15☽	16	17	18	19
20	21	22○	23	24	25	26
27	28☾	29	30			

July
Mon	Tues	Wed	Thur	Fri	Sat	Sun
				1	2	3
4	5	6●	7	8	9	10
11	12	13	14☽	15	16	17
18	19	20	21○	22	23	24
25	26	27	28☾	29	30	31

Aug
Mon	Tues	Wed	Thur	Fri	Sat	Sun
1	2	3	4	5●	6	7
8	9	10	11	12	13☽	14
15	16	17	18	19○	20	21
22	23	24	25	26☾	27	28
29	30	31				

Sept
Mon	Tues	Wed	Thur	Fri	Sat	Sun
			1	2	3●	4
5	6	7	8	9	10	11☽
12	13	14	15	16	17	18○
19	20	21	22	23	24	25☾
26	27	28	29	30		

Oct
Mon	Tues	Wed	Thur	Fri	Sat	Sun
					1	2
3●	4	5	6	7	8	9
10☽	11	12	13	14	15	16
17○	18	19	20	21	22	23
24	25☾	26	27	28	29	30
31						

Nov
Mon	Tues	Wed	Thur	Fri	Sat	Sun
	1	2●	3	4	5	6
7	8	9☽	10	11	12	13
14	15	16○	17	18	19	20
21	22	23☾	24	25	26	27
28	29	30				

Dec
Mon	Tues	Wed	Thur	Fri	Sat	Sun
			1●	2	3	4
5	6	7	8☽	9	10	11
12	13	14	15○	16	17	18
19	20	21	22	23☾	24	25
26	27	28	29	30	31●	

2006

Jan
Mon	Tues	Wed	Thur	Fri	Sat	Sun
						1
2	3	4	5	6☽	7	8
9	10	11	12	13	14○	15
16	17	18	19	20	21	22☾
23	24	25	26	27	28	29●
30	31					

Feb
Mon	Tues	Wed	Thur	Fri	Sat	Sun
		1	2	3	4	5☽
6	7	8	9	10	11	12
13○	14	15	16	17	18	19
20	21☾	22	23	24	25	26
27	28●					

Mar
Mon	Tues	Wed	Thur	Fri	Sat	Sun
		1	2	3	4	5
6☽	7	8	9	10	11	12
13	14○	15	16	17	18	19
20	21	22☾	23	24	25	26
27	28	29●	30	31		

Apr
Mon	Tues	Wed	Thur	Fri	Sat	Sun
					1	2
3	4	5☽	6	7	8	9
10	11	12	13○	14	15	16
17	18	19	20	21☾	22	23
24	25	26	27●	28	29	30

May
Mon	Tues	Wed	Thur	Fri	Sat	Sun
1	2	3	4	5☽	6	7
8	9	10	11	12	13○	14
15	16	17	18	19	20☾	21
22	23	24	25	26	27●	28
29	30	31				

June
Mon	Tues	Wed	Thur	Fri	Sat	Sun
			1	2	3☽	4
5	6	7	8	9	10	11○
12	13	14	15	16	17	18☾
19	20	21	22	23	24	25●
26	27	28	29	30		

July
Mon	Tues	Wed	Thur	Fri	Sat	Sun
					1	2
3☽	4	5	6	7	8	9
10	11○	12	13	14	15	16
17☾	18	19	20	21	22	23
24	25●	26	27	28	29	30
31						

Aug
Mon	Tues	Wed	Thur	Fri	Sat	Sun
	1	2☽	3	4	5	6
7	8	9○	10	11	12	13
14	15	16☾	17	18	19	20
21	22	23●	24	25	26	27
28	29	30	31☽			

Sept
Mon	Tues	Wed	Thur	Fri	Sat	Sun
				1	2	3
4	5	6	7○	8	9	10
11	12	13	14☾	15	16	17
18	19	20	21	22●	23	24
25	26	27	28	29	30☽	

Oct
Mon	Tues	Wed	Thur	Fri	Sat	Sun
						1
2	3	4	5	6	7○	8
9	10	11	12	13	14☾	15
16	17	18	19	20	21	22●
23	24	25	26	27	28	29☽
30	31					

Nov
Mon	Tues	Wed	Thur	Fri	Sat	Sun
		1	2	3	4	5○
6	7	8	9	10	11	12☾
13	14	15	16	17	18	19
20●	21	22	23	24	25	26
27	28☽	29	30			

Dec
Mon	Tues	Wed	Thur	Fri	Sat	Sun
				1	2	3
4	5○	6	7	8	9	10
11	12☾	13	14	15	16	17
18	19	20●	21	22	23	24
25	26	27☽	28	29	30	31

● New Moon   ☽ First Quarter   ○ Full Moon   ☾ Last Quarter

INTRODUCTION

Using the Book of Days

The Wicca Book of Days *is for those who want to know more about Wicca and for those who already follow the Old Religion.*

It explores the major Wiccan festivals and offers meditations to bring you into contact with the divine. Over the year you will encounter the three aspects of the Goddess. She appears as the Maiden in spring, Goddess of rejuvenation and reanimation; as the Mother in summer, who brings fruitfulness and creativity; and as the Crone in winter who shares her wisdom. You will also meet the young God in summer and the Horned God in winter.

As the year unfolds *The Book of Days* gives suggestions for celebrating the changing seasons and explores the magical elements and the witch's tools and offers practical ideas for magic and spell casting.

The Wicca Book of Days will evolve into a record of your personal magical journey. It will be a unique document of 'a year and a day' of magical work. You can use it to set down any dreams you feel are important and note your emotions through the changing seasons of the year. *The Book of Days* will become a chronicle of your individual magical aspirations and will help you to keep a check on whether you are achieving them.

You can also use *The Book of Days* to keep an accurate account of the spells you have cast. It is always a good idea to keep a record of the phase of the moon, the day, the time and the ingredients of your spell – you may want to repeat it some day. Most important of all, you will want to record how successful your spells were.

The Book of Days offers help in planning ahead for seasonal rites and the festival dates of goddesses and gods from various traditions are highlighted. There are recipes for incense, cakes and infusions for use during your sabbats.

Right: A Wiccan priestess and high priest exchange a ritual kiss.

What is Wicca?

Wicca is a spiritual path that centres on the worship of the divine in nature.

Wiccans believe that because every creature, rock and plant is part of the web of creation, every one of them is sacred. As a result, Wiccans revere nature and seek to protect the environment: they aim to watch over and to safeguard the land.

Unlike other Western religions, Wicca honours the Goddess as well as the God. Wiccans worship the great creative forces of the cosmos, in the form of the Mother Goddess and her son and consort. The Goddess shows us three faces, or aspects, during the waxing, full period and waning of each successive moon. These aspects are the Maiden, the Mother and the Crone and they symbolize the great archetypes of renewal, creation and wisdom. Wicca also venerates the Horned One, the God of life, death and resurrection. The Horned God of Wicca bears no relation to the Satan of Christianity. His horns signal his divine power and kinship with nature.

There are eight main festivals, or sabbats, in the Wiccan calendar. Tied to the changing seasons, these festivals are: Samhain (31 October), Winter Solstice (21/22 December), Imbolc (1/2 February), the Spring Equinox (21/22 March), Beltane (30 April/1 May), Midsummer Solstice (21/22 June), Lammas (31 July/1 August) and the Autumn Equinox (21/22 September). Wiccans celebrate at night, so Wiccan festivals start in the evening and carry on until the next day. Wiccans celebrate each full moon at an esbat ritual.

Celebrating the various sabbats and esbats of the year keeps Wiccans in close contact with the rhythms of the earth. They learn to respond to the changing tides of energy as the year turns through its cycle.

Left: A Wiccan high priestess prepares herself for a water meditation.

January

In January many Wiccans spend time looking back on the year that has just ended and considering the year to come. They make space for quiet reflection every day.

Everyone can learn to meditate with a little practice. Try to be consistent: five minutes at the same time each day is far more useful than trying to meditate for half an hour once a week.

Make yourself comfortable and relax. Close your eyes and breathe deeply, letting all the stress of the day fade away. Concentrate on your breathing. Feel each in breath fill you with cleansing energy and each out breath rid you of negativity and tension. Allow your mind to become still.

Activate your seven energy points, or chakras. They revitalize and empower you by opening your spirit to the energy of the earth. The base chakra is located at the base of the spine; the sacral chakra is just below the navel; the solar plexus chakra is just above the navel; the heart chakra is in the middle of the chest; the throat chakra is at the throat; the third eye chakra is in the middle of the forehead; and the crown chakra is at the top of the head. The base and crown chakras remain slightly open at all times, connecting us with the cosmos.

Feel the great pulse of energy rising from the earth. Sense your base chakra opening wide and your coccyx area filling with crimson light. When this area is overflowing with light, allow your sacral chakra to open and a warm orange glow to fill that area. Allow your other chakras to open in turn, filling you with golden light (solar plexus), emerald light (heart), blue light (throat) and violet light (third eye). When your chakras are open and your body is filled with earth energy, allow this to spill out through your crown chakra in a stream of brilliant white.

When you have finished meditating, close your chakras in reverse order, leaving the crown and base chakras slightly open.

Far Left: A Wiccan priestess allows earth energy to flood through her before beginning a ritual. *Below:* Open your chakras before meditation to connect you with the energy of the earth and the heavens.

JANUARY 1 - 7

January 1

Festival of Hera, the Greek queen of heaven.

Festival of Chronos, father of time.

January 2

Birthday of Inanna, Sumerian goddess of the Underworld.

January 3

January 4

January 5

January 6

Festival of the Triple Goddess.

January 7

Greek feast of Persephone.

Festival of Isis as protector of children begins.

Magic to do with initiating plans and expansion should coincide with the waxing phase of the moon. Magic for completion and fulfilment should

Goal-Setting Meditation

Spend the quiet period after Yule planning what you hope to achieve, both magically and practically, during the coming year. It's a good idea to schedule new projects, creative activities and financial ventures between now and the Midsummer Solstice, while the energizing power of the sun is on the increase. Study projects are better undertaken towards the end of the year, when our focus turns inwards.

Developing your psychic, intuitive and magical skills can be undertaken at any time but it is best to organize magical work to coincide with the appropriate phases of the waxing and full moon.

be timed for the full moon and magic aimed at ridding yourself of problems should be undertaken during the waning phase of the moon.

JANUARY 8 - 14

January 8

Festival of Isis as protector of children ends.

January 9

Festival of Janus, guardian of the gateways.

January 10

January 11

January 12

January 13

January 14

Make a reviving wassail cup to share with friends. Heat some cider or apple juice and add a few baked apples, drizzled with honey, to the pan.

Wassailing

Remember the ancient ceremony of wassailing if you have apple trees in your garden. On 6 or 17 January make an offering of cider to the roots of the tree and hang some apple cake or toast soaked in cider from the branches. Make a loud noise with cymbals, drums or rattles to drive away any evil spirits, and sing to your tree to ensure a large crop. In the south of England, apple trees are still serenaded with this traditional song:

Old apple tree, old apple tree,
We've come to wassail thee,
To bear and to bow, apples anow,
Hats full, caps full and three bushel
bags full,
Barn floors full and a little heap
under the stairs, Hurrah!

JANUARY 15 - 21

January 15

January 16

January 17

January 18

January 19

January 20

January 21

'I shall go into a hare, with sorrow and sighing and mickle care.'

Traditional

Shape Shifting

Witches have always been credited
with the ability to change form
and assume the shape of a cat,
wolf or, more often, a hare.
Nowadays Wiccans still try to
connect with animal spirits to
extend their understanding of
their fellow creatures.

Lie comfortably and open your
chakras. Concentrate on the
animal you wish to contact. Allow
your mind's eye to search the
countryside until it sees the right
animal. Ask permission of the
creature and, if you are welcome,
allow your consciousness to
merge with that of the animal.
See what it sees, hear what it
hears and move as it moves. You
will know when the time is right
to return. Thank the animal and
slowly return to your body. Eat
something to ground yourself.

JANUARY 22 - 28

January 22

Greek festival of the Muses, goddesses of creative inspiration.
Feast of Apollo.

January 23

January 24

Festival of Thoth begins.

January 25

January 26

Sacred to Cernunnos and popular as a day of initiation.

January 27

Festival of Thoth ends.

January 28

In the Scottish highlands, married women would make a bed for Brigid next to the hearth.

Making a Brigid's Cross

It's time to make preparations for Imbolc. In honour of Brigid, the Maiden, who returns to earth each spring, try making a traditional symbol of the Goddess.

To create a simple Brigid's Cross, gather four bunches of reeds of the same length and thickness (or buy sea grass from a craft shop). Fold the first bunch in half and flatten it; secure the loose ends together with red thread. Fold your second bunch of stems through the first loop, at a 90-degree angle (about $^2/_3$ of the way along the bunch) and secure the ends. Fold the third through the second in the same way. Take your last bunch and fold over the third bunch as before, but push these loose ends through the empty loop of the first bunch before tying them neatly.

They would decorate it with ribbons and place a bundle of reeds in the centre to symbolize the Goddess.

February

Imbolc marks the return of the Goddess to the land. After her sojourn in the underworld she has renewed herself and appears as a virgin once more.

The homecoming of the Goddess is heralded by the pale, white light of the lengthening days and by the first fragile green shoots to emerge from the snow. At Imbolc the Goddess is welcomed in her Maiden aspect: as a young girl, gentle and innocent of the world. Imbolc was originally a Celtic fertility festival. Imbolc or Oimelc (meaning 'ewes' milk') celebrated the coming into lactation of the flocks. This period was also sacred to Brigid, the radiant goddess of fertility and fire. Brigid was associated with the whiteness of milk, the brilliance of flame, and the purity of snow. Her shining presence is still honoured today in the spotless white dresses of brides. At Imbolc, witches acknowledge the power of the Goddess to transform and to make new. Glowing candles fill Wiccan circles with warmth and light and altars are decorated with fresh young snowdrops and budding twigs. It is common to undertake magical work connected with renewal or regeneration and early spring rituals are infused with a sense of new life and optimism. Imbolc is also the time when witches customarily begin their spring-cleaning. This old tradition recognizes the need to rid the home of the last vestiges of the dankness and gloom of winter. With spring-cleaning, witches consecrate and prepare their homes for the year to come.

Far Left: A Wiccan high priestess wears the crescent moon of the virgin goddess of spring.

Below: At Imbolc Wiccans light candles to symbolize the return of the light after winter.

JANUARY 29 – FEBRUARY 4

January 29

January 30

Roman festival of peace, in honour of the goddess Pax.

January 31

February 1

Imbolc.

Greek festival of Dionysus begins.

February 2

Egyptian festival of Nuit.

Feast of Celtic goddess Brigid.

February 3

February 4

In ancient Rome, priests greatly revered sage as a herb which cleansed both mind and body. Priests

Earth Chalice Spell

Winter is associated with the element of earth, which rules balance and wisdom. This spell stimulates your practicality and enhances your perception. It should be carried out under a waxing moon.

Place your pentacle in the base of a cauldron. Place two cups of hot water in the cauldron and add a teaspoon each of dried sage and honey and a pinch of dried lavender flowers. Stir the brew deosil (clockwise) with your black-handled knife while it infuses. Transfer to a chalice. As you drink, chant quietly:

Beat of the heart, pulse of the earth
Give my understanding birth.
Pulse of the earth, beat of the heart
Bring wisdom to my art.

Sip the brew while studying or to enhance your wisdom.

would approach the plant on their knees and gather leaves only after they had made offerings of wine and bread.

FEBRUARY 5 - 11

February 5

Celtic festival of wyrd (auspicious time for divination).

February 6

Festival of Greek goddess Aphrodite.

February 7

February 8

February 9

February 10

February 11

Egyptian festival of Osiris begins.

'She is the bright huntress, queen of beasts,
She runs with the wolf and with the lion
For She is the protector, She of the crescent moon.'

Maiden Meditation

Relax, breathe deeply and allow your mind to become still. Open your chakras. Find yourself in a moonlit grove. The air is cool and a steady breeze blows in from the east. As you walk, you see a silver light ahead. You follow the path until you reach a clearing and there, in the middle, you find the Maiden. She is bright and shining in the moonlight. She stands tall and straight, her body poised as if ready for flight. She is crowned with flowers and a white crescent moon sits on her forehead.

Approach her. You may be given a gift, for hers is the ability to make new, to revitalize and to bring life and growth.

When you are ready, thank the Maiden and return to your everyday consciousness. Eat something to ground yourself.

FEBRUARY 12 - 18

February 12

February 13

Egyptian festival of Osiris ends.

Start of Lupercalia, Roman festival in honour of Faunus (Roman Pan), protector of flocks.

February 14

Greek festival of Dionysus ends.

February 15

Lupercalia ends.

February 16

February 17

February 18

Anoint your candles with a few drops of clary sage essential oil to improve your clairvoyance, lavender for personal balance or hazelnut oil for wisdom.

Candle Spells

A candle spell is one of the easiest ways to begin making magic. Choose a colour to match your intent. Blue and purple are often used to improve psychic abilities, red is for passion and energy, pink for friendship, green for love, luck and abundance, white to increase spiritual awareness and black to rid yourself of negative energy.

Empower your candle by carving onto it the crescent moon of the Goddess and the eight-spoked sun-wheel of the God. Consecrate it by passing it through salt, water, incense smoke and the flame of an altar candle. As you do this, concentrate on the magic you hope to achieve. Burn the candle for an hour each day and use that time to reaffirm your magical intent.

FEBRUARY 19 - 25

February 19

February 20

February 21

February 22

Roman feast of Concordia, goddess of goodwill and forgiveness.

February 23

February 24

February 25

Daisy is a corruption of 'day's eye' as the flowers open in the morning and close at night. The custom of pulling off the petals while reciting

Clear-Sight Potion

This potion can be used both to soothe the eyes and to improve 'inner vision'.

Bring two cups of spring water to the boil. To it, add a teaspoon of fresh or dried angelica leaves and a teaspoon of fresh or dried daisy petals. Stir the mixture deosil using a wand. Add a teaspoon of honey to this mix and drink it as a refreshing tea, or allow it to cool and drink it during divination.

To clear your sight, dip some pads of cotton wool in the cold potion and apply it to your closed eyes. Leave the pads in place and spend ten minutes meditating. Your eyes will be refreshed and your insight strengthened.

'she loves me, she loves me not' gave the daisy its folk name, 'measure of love.'

March

On 21 March the Vernal, or Spring, Equinox marks the true beginning of spring.

At the equinox, one of the major turning points of the year, day and night rest in equilibrium for a few days before the light begins to exert its power and the days really begin to lengthen.

This festival is also known as Ostara and marks the return of vegetation to the land. March is traditionally a time of seed sowing: of developing ideas and plans. Wiccans celebrate the impregnation of the Goddess by the young, virile God. The return to the land of the Goddess is confirmed by the growth of green shoots and fresh flowers. In one sense, the Goddess can be seen as the land waiting for the plough. The ever-strengthening sun has warmed the soil and it is time to sow the seed.

Traditional fertility symbols at this time of year are the hare and the egg. The hare has long been revered for its magical connections and its impressive fertility. We can still recognize the hare today in Easter celebrations, transformed and sentimentalized as the 'Easter Bunny'.

The symbolism of the egg is twofold. On one level it is simply a domestic sign that spring has arrived and that hens will begin to lay once again. On another, it is a magic symbol of the cosmic 'world egg', or originator of life. The Goddess, as ultimate creatrix, carries the egg with her to show her creative power.

Wiccans invariably honour the impregnation of the Goddess by planting a seed. In ritual, they infuse the seed with the energy of their hopes and plans for the coming summer. As the seed germinates and then grows, so they hope their plans will also grow to fulfilment.

Far Left: Ostara, goddess of fertility, holds the cosmic egg, a symbol of her power.
Left: Wiccans decorate their altars with eggs in honour of the Goddess.

FEBRUARY 26 - MARCH 4

February 26

February 27

February 28

March 1

Roman Matoronalia, festival of Juno, protector of women.

March 2

Roman festival of Vesta, goddess of the fire of purification.

March 3

March 4

Violets are sacred to the goddess Aphrodite and were symbols of fertility to the Ancient

Air Elemental Incense

Spring is associated with the element of Air. To contact the element, bring inspiration and stimulate the mind, try making this air incense:

3 parts balm of Gilead buds
4 parts copal resin
3 parts benzoin resin
3 parts dried lavender flowers
1 part dried violet petals
$1/2$ part dried apple blossom
9 drops frankincense oil
1 part wine, honey, olive oil mix

Grind the dry ingredients together in a pestle and mortar until you have a fine powder. Mix to a sticky consistency with the frankincense and wine, honey and oil mixture. Store in an airtight container. Burn on charcoal discs in a well-insulated censer.

Greeks. Their energy helps us slip into the 'space between the worlds'.

MARCH 5 - 11

March 5

March 6   Festival of Mars, Roman god of war.

March 7

March 8

March 9

March 10

March 11

Dyeing eggs for your equinox rites is easy. Simply boil white eggs with beetroot to produce pink,

Ostara

Ostara, also known as Eostre, was a pagan goddess of fertility. Easter, the Christian festival, which lies near the spring equinox, derives its name and its symbols from her. The Easter egg, for example, was originally Ostara's emblem, a sign of her wholeness and unfailing fertility. Such was the power of her fertility that oestrogen, the hormone that prompts egg production in women, is named after her. Ostara's arrival was marked by the blossoming of yellow flowers such as primroses and daffodils and by the fresh green leaves. Wiccans decorate eggs to honour Ostara.

In Britain folk customs connected with hunting for eggs or rolling eggs persist – vestiges of pagan fertility rites dedicated to Ostara, goddess of the spring.

with onion-skins to make brown eggs and with gorse petals for beautiful yellow eggs.

MARCH 12 - 18

March 12

March 13

March 14

March 15

March 16

Dionysia, festival in honour of the Greek god Dionysus, begins.

March 17

March 18

A Call to Pan
'Io Pan, Io Pan, Io Pan, Pan Pan!'

Pan

With the coming of spring, the young Horned God comes to strength and power. The young God seeks out the Goddess, woos her and impregnates her. In doing so he fulfils the role of both hunter and agricultural fertility symbol. His pursuit and capture of the Goddess mirrors the hunt, while his impregnation of the Goddess reflects the ploughing and sowing of the land.

Many Wiccans have adopted the Greek deity Pan as a symbol of the Horned God's virility and life-affirming lust. The ancient Greeks knew Pan as 'He who eats all; He who begets all'. In spring, Wiccans decorate altars in honour of Pan. They place antlers, which symbolize strength and masculine energy, on the altar and drape them with fresh greenery.

MARCH 19 - 25

Match 19
Dionysia, festival in honour of the god Dionysus, ends.

Match 20

Match 21
Spring Equinox.

Match 22

Match 23

Match 24

Match 25

'As the wind and weather at the Equinox,
So they will be for the next three months.'
Traditional

Planting a Seed

Many Wiccans plant seeds at this time of year, in a symbolic re-creation of the impregnation of the Goddess.

First choose your seed. If you want your seed to sprout, no matter what, pick something easy to grow like mustard and cress, sunflowers or lettuce. Choosing edible plants means you can eat the leaves when they have grown and thus take the magical intent back into your body.

Fill a small pot with potting compost. Ask the blessings of the Gods on your plans and allow their energy to infuse the seeds. Plant your seeds, water them and tend them until they grow to maturity. If your new plant produces seeds of its own, keep these until the next spring equinox and plant them then.

April

In northern Europe, April is the month traditionally associated with ploughing.

The patron saint of England, St George, famed for his prowess as a dragon slayer, also has an ancient pagan connection to the plough. In Greek the name George translates as ploughman and in some countries he is known as 'Green George', the protector of the plough. St George's day falls on 23 April and traditionally marks the beginning of the cultivation of the fields.

St George cries Go!
St Mark cries Hoe!   (Traditional)

In some folk traditions it is taboo to sit on the ground in winter because the earth is not 'breathing' and therefore is considered poisonous. The coming of spring and the ploughing of the land is believed to drive out any corruption left in the ground. In some countries it is still considered good luck to kill snakes (symbols of the underworld and of winter), provided this is done in the period before spring arrives. It is interesting that St George, ploughman and herald of spring, is also famous for killing a serpent-like dragon. It seems that his role is to make the land fertile by ploughing it, thus destroying the barrenness of winter. He can be seen as a surviving pagan fertility symbol: as someone who furrows the land and in doing so, impregnates the Goddess.

In Scotland the first Friday of April was commonly known as the 'Witches' Sabbath'. It was believed that this Friday was chosen in honour of the Norse fertility goddess Frigga, who gave her name to the day. Frigga was demonized by the early Christian church fathers and was thought to take her revenge on Fridays, which were widely believed to be unlucky days for Christians, who had ousted her from power.

According to traditional wisdom in England, the cuckoo sings for the first time of the year on 14 April, ushering in spring.

Left: A Wiccan priestess calls to the spirit of the woods.

MARCH 26 - APRIL 1

March 26

March 27

March 28

March 29

March 30   Feast of Ostara, fertility goddess.

March 31   Festival of Isis as queen of the moon.

April 1   Norse festival of Loki, the trickster god.

'A new moon with sharp horns threatens windy weather.'
Traditional

New Moon

When the newly waxing moon reaches its first quarter, it forms the silver crescent of the Goddess in her Maiden aspect. The 'horns' of a waxing moon always face the left. It is considered disrespectful to point at the new moon, so many witches bow instead.

An old country custom states that if you make a wish and bow nine times to the new moon your wish will come true. Other traditions say that when you first see the new moon, you should turn over any silver coins you have in your pockets. Doing this will ensure your prosperity for the next month.

Country people believe that if the new moon rises bright and yellow in the sky there will be several days of good weather.

APRIL 2 - 8

april 2

april 3

april 4

april 5

The 'Witches' Sabbath', sacred to Frigga.

april 6

april 7

april 8

*Sacred to Aphrodite and Venus, the rose symbolizes
female mystery. Oak represents male power.*

Beltane Incense

This heady, sensual incense is perfect at Beltane to honour the marriage of the Goddess and God. Make it now and allow it to mature. Create your incense on a Friday, while the moon is waxing.

3 parts benzoin resin
4 parts copal resin
3 parts lavender flowers
1 part rose petals
9 drops amber oil
9 drops rose oil
9 drops frankincense oil
3 drops oak moss oil
1 part wine, honey, olive oil mix

Grind the resins to a fine powder in a pestle and mortar, then stir in the petals, the oils and the wine, honey and oil mix. Burn on charcoal disks in a censer during your Beltane celebrations.

Combined, these plants make a perfect symbol of the marriage of the Gods.

APRIL 9 - 15

April 9

April 10

April 11

April 12

April 13 — Festival of Ceres, Roman goddess of grain.

April 14

April 15

*Green is the colour of rejuvenation, of energy,
and of fertility. When the woods and forests are*

Energy Spell

As the power of the sun increases and the land begins to turn green once again, Wiccans often cast spells for rejuvenation and renewed energy.

Half fill a glass chalice or goblet with white wine or spring water. To this add a large spoon of honey (or piece of honeycomb), a twist of lemon peel, the juice of half a lemon, and a large pinch of grated ginger.

Hold the chalice in the sunlight, against a background of trees and bushes. Allow the green light to fill the chalice and chant:

Green restore and green quicken
Ever prosper, never sicken
Green revive and green renew
This with energy imbue!

Drink the potion over the course of the day, and feel it revive you and bring you spring energy.

green, it signifies the rising of the sap and the return of life and vitality to the earth.

APRIL 16 - 22

April 16

April 17

April 18

April 19

April 20

April 21

April 22

The pinecone-tipped wand is an emblem of male potency. It is used in many Wiccan rites to exemplify the fertilizing power of the sun.

Making a Wand

With the summer getting closer and the sap rising in the trees, now is a good time to fashion a new wand. Wands are associated with the element of Fire and so can be made in the full light of the sun. At midday, find an appropriate tree (ash and oak are seen as masculine, willow and rowan as feminine). Ask permission of the tree and, if permitted, choose a thin branch, about as long as your forearm. Make one quick, clean cut, thank the tree and leave it an offering.

At home, peel back the outer bark and oil the wood to make it smooth. You can paint symbols and runes on your wand to increase its power or add a crystal to one end to help you direct energy more efficiently.

APRIL 23 - 29

April 23

April 24

April 25

April 26

April 27

April 28

Roman festival of Floralia, a celebration of Flora, goddess of flowers.

April 29

'Mist in May, Heat in June, Make the harvest come right soon.'

Traditional

Garlands of Green

May eve is almost here, the time when male and female witches make garlands of fresh flowers and leaves to wear in their hair to celebrate the marriage of the God and Goddess.

For a Goddess crown, gather bunches of blossom (remember, only pick hawthorn on May eve itself) and tie these around a chaplet of twined ivy. If you can't get fresh blossom, buy roses, freesias or lilies from a florist.

For an Oak King garland, tie bunches of fresh, young oak leaves around a crown of twisted honeysuckle. Keep tying in leaves until you have a thick, verdant ring of oak. If oak is still scarce you can add leaves from other trees associated with the God, such as ash, hazel or bay.

May

Beltane falls on May eve and is the most sensual of all the sabbats: a loving celebration of the tenderness and mystery of sexual union and fulfilment.

When the earth is at its most lush, green and beautiful, Wiccans honour the union of the gods; the coming together of the primal creativity of the earth and the fertilizing power of the sun.

Beltane means 'the fire of Bel', the Celtic sun god, and the festival marked the beginning of the ancient Celtic summer. Cattle were released to their summer pastures and were driven through the smoke of Bel 'tans', or fires, to purify and cleanse them. Wiccans mark this festival by lighting their own Bel fires and leaping through the flames to ensure prosperity for the coming season. In the recent past, every village lad and lass would go 'a-Maying'. This was, in theory, a trip into the woods on May eve to gather blossom with which to decorate the maypole. In reality it meant an evening of sexual abandon under the stars. Couples would pair off in the dark, sometimes not knowing the identity of their partners. These short-term sexual liaisons were called 'Greenwood marriages'. Any unexpected children who arrived as a result of the Beltane revels were often named Robinson or Godkin after their supposed father, the legendary Robin Goodfellow, the Lord of the Woods.

Going 'a-Maying' echoed and may actually have constituted the last vestiges of earlier Pagan fertility rites. Participants would have re-enacted, in human terms, the sexual union of the gods at this time of year. Such rites were originally accepted as natural and were considered essential to fully protect the fertility of the land.

Today Wiccans celebrate Beltane with rituals that express the joy of this time of year.

Far Left: A Beltane crown, left in the woods as an offering of thanks to the gods.
Below: Wiccan priests 'capture' a priestess to be 'Queen of the May', consort of the Oak King.

APRIL 30 - MAY 6

April 30

May 1

Beltane.

Festival of Isis.

Festival of Vulcan and all smiths.

May 2

May 3

May 4

May 5

May 6

With its long magical history, hawthorn has many folk names. Descriptions such as heathenberry,

Hawthorn Garlands

Wiccan priestesses wear garlands and crowns of hawthorn blossom in order to honour the great Goddess during their Beltane rites. Hawthorn flowers symbolize female mystery and fertility and, among Wiccans, the plant is traditionally believed to be so magically potent that it is considered unlucky to cut it or to bring it inside the house except on May eve, when hawthorn is used to deck the Beltane altar.

For May blossom magic, pick a branch of hawthorn blossom by the light of the Beltane moon. Infuse some of the petals in water or wine, inhale the perfume of the flowers and drink in the mystery of the Goddess.

pixie-pear, hegpeg, moonflower and, most tellingly,
hagthorn, warn the uninitiated of the plant's power.

MAY 7 - 13

May 7

May 8

May 9

May 10

May 11

May 12

May 13

Shaft's Court, in central London, got its name from
the huge maypole, or shaft, erected there every May
Day. The pole once rose higher than the local

The Maypole

The maypole symbolizes the union of male and female, the Goddess and God. The upright, phallic pole represents the potency of the God and his ability to make fertile the land. The pole is traditionally topped with a ring of flowers, representing the Goddess. At one time, every village had a maypole, and some were kept permanently in place to ensure luck and prosperity.

Most covens include maypole dances in their Beltane rites. Coven members dance back and forth, weaving coloured ribbons around the central pole. As they dance, they tie the abundance of the coming summer into the ribbons. Some covens keep the maypole tied until the following year, others dance outwards again, releasing the fertility and luck.

church steeple and the church became known as
St Andrews-under-the-Shaft.

MAY 14 - 20

May 14

May 15

May 16

May 17

May 18

May 19

May 20

'With a Hal-an-tow! Rumbelow!
For we are up as soon as any day O,
And for to fetch the summer home,

HandFasting

Many Wiccans choose to celebrate their own marriages between Beltane and the Summer Solstice in June. Wiccan marriages are known as 'handfastings'. In the ceremony the couple's hands are ritually bound together to symbolize their union.

Traditionally, a handfasted couple would make a commitment to one another for the magical period of a year and a day. The ceremony was sealed when they jumped over a broomstick. In Britain, to this day, some people refer to unmarried couples who live together as living 'over the broom'. Modern Wiccans customarily treat their handfasting with the same gravity as any other wedding ceremony and see it as a commitment for life.

The summer and the May O,
The summer is a come O,
And the winter is a gone O.' Traditional

MAY 21 - 27

May 21

May 22

May 23

May 24

May 25

May 26

May 27

In the middle ages, sweet woodruff (galium odoratum)
was traditionally added to white wine to create the

Aphrodisiac Cup

Half fill a large punch bowl with crushed ice. Cover the ice with a layer of sliced strawberries or any other summer fruit. Add a good sprinkling of icing sugar and a slosh of brandy. Pour a bottle of champagne over the ice. For a strictly non-alcoholic version, choose sparkling fruit juice or soda instead.

Float fresh flowers on the surface. Roses, pansies, violets, daisies, cottage pinks and borage are all completely edible. Fill a large chalice or goblet from the punch bowl, making sure there are some flowers floating in it. Serve your aphrodisiac cup to the guests at your seasonal celebrations. Everyone should drink from the same goblet, passing from male to female to male with a kiss.

May bowl. Steep a handful of fresh or dried leaves in the wine overnight, chill and drink on May Day.

June

June heralds the height of the summer sun: the longest day and shortest night of the year fall on the Summer Solstice, on 21 June.

Midsummer is a time of ease and plenty, when plans have time to evolve and ideas blossom. Wiccans rejoice in the strength of the sun at its most powerful. They celebrate the God's strength while remembering that even this is transitory and must pass. Just as the shortest day at Yule brought the promise of light to come, so the longest day brings shorter evenings and a withdrawing of the sun's power.

Over the last century, pagans and, in particular, Druids have celebrated the solstice at Britain's most well-known stone circle, Stonehenge. Stonehenge remains a site of spectacular power, enduring and untouched by the passing of time. The stones are laid out to form a complex pattern of criss-cross alignments which mark the rising and setting of the sun and the moon at different times of the year. The most famous of these is the Midsummer sunrise over the hele (or heel) stone, which many believe marks the original processional way into the circle. The sun rises behind the stone, casting a phallic shaft of shadow into the womb-like centre of the circle. Just before dawn, the Druids process from the hele stone into the circle to perform their solstice rite.

Recent research has also shown that the circular layout of upright stones at the centre of the henge amplifies any sounds that are produced there. The noise of chanting or drumming at the centre of the circle appears to be augmented by the stones and broadcast to the outer ring. This new discovery lends credence to the theory that Stonehenge was used as a ritual site as well as an astronomical observatory.

Whatever its original purpose, Stonehenge has once again become a focal point for modern pagan celebrations.

Left: A Wiccan priest greets the dawn at Stonehenge.

MAY 28 - JUNE 3

May 28

May 29

May 30

May 31

June 1

June 2

June 3

'He is the lord of the wild wood, the running one,
He is the lord of the moor and of the forest floor
He is hunter, hunted: slayer, slain.'

Oak-Tree Meditation

As the Summer Solstice draws near, the power of the God is reaching its zenith. This is an ideal time to contact the spirit of the woods. At noon on a sunny day, sit with your back against an oak tree. Feel the trunk supporting you. Experience the power of the tree.

Imagine yourself sinking backwards through a doorway in the tree trunk. You may find yourself deep in the forest, the sun dappling through a thick canopy of leaves. Look around: you might see a horned figure flickering through the branches. Spend some time in the heart of the wood.

After your encounter with the lord of the greenwood, thank the oak tree and offer a libation of food or wine at its roots.

JUNE 4 - 10

June 4

June 5

June 6

June 7

June 8

June 9   Vestalia, Roman festival of purification in honour of Vesta.

June 10

After every meditation, remember to eat and drink something to ground yourself after your journey.

Encountering the Earth Mother

This exercise is best carried out in your garden. Otherwise choose a place where the moonlight penetrates indoors. Under the light of a full moon, lie or sit on the earth, where you will be bathed in moonlight.

Become aware of the great Mother Earth as she supports your body. Allow yourself to sink into her embrace. Feel the rocks and soil under your fingertips. Smell the sweet scent of the earth. As you sink deep into the arms of the Mother, listen to sounds of creation all around you. Seeds are germinating and sending up shoots. Plants and trees push their roots deep into the earth and she never fails to support and nurture them.

You may like to offer some bread or wine as a libation to the Goddess to thank her for her presence.

JUNE 11 - 17

June 11

June 12

June 13

June 14

June 15

June 16

June 17

'Cut off my head and I will louder sing,
The song of the woods and of the spring.
Cut off my head and I live always,

Green Man

While the term 'green man' was coined for the first time in 1939, the symbol is an ancient one and dates back at least as far as classical Rome, where foliate heads were common symbols of fertility. The green man is a pagan image found in wood or stone carvings in many medieval churches and buildings across Europe.

In England he is known as Jack-in-the-Green, in France, Le Feuillou or Le Loup Vert, and in Bavaria, Pfingstl. Whatever his name, his appearance is the same, a face or whole body, made up of verdant foliage, marking him as the spirit of the woods. In English churches only the face is shown, mouth open, with stems thrusting outwards in an ancient phallic gesture.

Ever stronger, green limbs ablaze.
I am the heart of the wild, the green man says.'

JUNE 18 - 24

June 18

June 19

June 20

June 21

Midsummer Solstice.

June 22

June 23

June 24

During the eighteenth and nineteenth centuries women would wear belts and garlands of mugwort

Greeting the Solstice Dawn

Midsummer marks the longest day of the year and the height of the sun's power. Many witches sit in vigil round the fire on the night of 21 June, waiting for the solstice dawn to rise. Some traditions 'sing the sun up', chanting, drumming and dancing to encourage the sun to rise.

If you wait to greet the solstice dawn you can make a toast to the sun as it rises. Fill a large glass jug or goblet with spring water and hold it above your head to catch the light of the rising sun. When your goblet is filled with light, say:

Let this chalice be filled with light and life and love
May all who drink from it be filled with the same.

at midsummer celebrations. These were thrown into the fire to bring good luck to the wearer.

July

The Saxons knew July as Lida oeftevr (the mild month). July brings the long, warm evenings of summer, perfect for outdoor meditations and rites.

Whenever possible, Wiccans cast their circles and make magic under the light of the moon. The moon is seen as feminine, balancing and introspective, with the power to synthesize and create harmony. While the moon is waxing, Wiccans cast spells of expansion and increase. This could cover an individual witch's hopes of improving her finances or her desire for greater magical skill or knowledge.

The full moon is usually reserved for magic that promotes a greater understanding of the gods or allows access to deeper levels of intuition. Intuition is seen by many as a 'gift of the Goddess' and is more easily accessible in moonlight. Spells of decrease and banishment are most often undertaken during the waning moon. This is the traditional time to rid yourself of fears, weaknesses and negative influences. Many witches suspend their spell craft and rest during the dark of the moon.

The moon also rules the element of Water. Sacred wells and springs have always been associated with symbolic rebirth. Swallowhead Spring, for example, which runs past the sacred site of Silbury Hill, Wiltshire, England, regularly dries up in winter, when tradition has it that the Goddess sleeps. Around February the stream starts flowing again, marking the return of the Goddess to the earth.

By association, the cauldron and chalice symbolize the womb of rebirth, creativity and change; both are used for the blending of healing potions. A cauldron or chalice is present in every Wiccan rite, embodying female energy. During the rite, the athame (symbol of male energy) is plunged into the chalice of wine as a re-enactment of the sexual union of the gods.

Left: A Wiccan priestess pours a libation of water in honour of the Goddess.

JUNE 25 - JULY 1

June 25

June 26

June 27

June 28

June 29

June 30

July 1

July is dedicated to the Babylonian goddess Ishtar.

Rosemary cleanses and repels any negative thoughts; thyme protects and helps you to focus,

The Dreaming Bath

Warm summer evenings are the perfect time for exploring your dreams. Try this old recipe, which helps you to 'dream true', in your bath before you go to bed.

Infuse sprigs of fresh rosemary, lavender and thyme in a bowl of hot water, then scatter a handful of fresh, red rose petals and poppy seeds over the surface. Allow the mixture to infuse for an hour, then strain. Before you bathe, light some rose-scented candles, then add your infusion to a warm bath and sink into the water.

Carry the energy of your potion with you to bed and allow yourself to drift off into a blissful dream state. In the morning, be sure to make a note of any dreams you have had.

while lavender brings inner stillness. Rose petals and poppy seeds will help to activate your intuitive power.

JULY 2 - 8

July 2

July 3

July 4

July 5

July 6

July 7

July 8

There are many goddesses of the moon, among them Aine, Artemis, Belili, Ceridwen, Diana, Hathor and Hecate.

Full Moon

Floating luminous, pearl-white and perfect against an indigo sky, the full moon in summer expresses the power of the Goddess. Sacred to Inanna (Queen of the Moon), and Pasiphae (She who Shines for All), the moon rules time and tide. The full moon is the most powerful time for magical work.

Try 'moon raking' by catching the moon's light in a chalice. Angle your goblet until the moon is reflected in the water. Feel the power of the Goddess pouring into your cup and filling it with silver light. Sip the water and allow the strength of the Goddess to flood your being. Use this water to consecrate space, or pour it into your bath and bathe in the radiance of the Goddess.

JULY 9 - 15

July 9

July 10

July 11

July 12

July 13

July 14

July 15

To make a magical tea to drink during your
consecration rite, add three teaspoons of rose and

Moonbeam Oil

Find a clear glass jar or bottle with a tight-fitting stopper. Fill it to the top with a mixture of fresh rose and jasmine petals, packing them in as tightly as possible. Fill the bottle with organic sweet almond oil. Tap the bottle to get rid of any air bubbles, then seal it. Place your bottle where it will be bathed in moonlight and leave it there from the new moon until the moon is full. Both rose and jasmine enhance intuitive capabilities, while the light of the moon deepens psychic awareness.

Strain out the flowers and keep your moon-charged oil in a cool, dark place. You can use your moonbeam oil for anointing ritual tools, jewellery, talismans, crystals and yourself.

jasmine petals and a teaspoon of honey to a cup of hot water. Dried petals can be bought from herbal suppliers.

JULY 16 - 22

July 16

July 17

July 18

July 19

July 20

July 21

July 22

Keep your pyrite egg near you whenever you need to stimulate your creativity. Place it on your altar to infuse your rites with creative energy.

Creativity Spell

At full moon cleanse a pyrite crystal by soaking it in salt water overnight. To increase your creativity, pour a ring of rock salt onto a flat surface. Say:

May the cleansing power of earth drive away all hindrances to my creativity.

Next, place a ring of fresh oak leaves over the ring of salt. Say:

May the creative power of the Lord of Life fill this circle.

Pour a circle of honey, saying:

May the sweetness of the Goddess fill this circle.

Place your pyrite egg over your heart chakra and say:

By the powers of the mighty ones of the elements, by the Lord of Life and the Great Goddess, may my creativity grow and blossom. So mote it be!

Balance the pyrite in the centre on a pile of salt and leave for the period of the full moon.

JULY 23 - 29

July 23

July 24

July 25

July 26

July 27

July 28

July 29

The spiral, emblem of the goddess, symbolizes the ebb a[nd]
flow of energy through each month and through the yea[r]

Moon Bathing

Women who wish to create a closer connection with the Goddess should bathe in the light of the moon at least once a month. Sit or lie in bright moonlight, with your skin in contact with the earth. This is particularly useful for women who have irregular periods and may help your body regulate menstruation.

Some witches sit on the ground during their period and allow their blood to return to the earth in an offering of thanks to the Goddess. This powerful act reconnects the body with ancient tides of regeneration and rebirth. Moon bathing can also help men achieve a better understanding of the Goddess. To gain knowledge of the God, bathe in sunlight (taking care not to get burned).

August

Lammas, Loaf mass or the Feast of First Fruits, is celebrated on 1 August, the time of the early harvest.

Witches decorate their altars with sheaves of grain, bowls of fruit and poppies. As the blackberries ripen and the reaping of the harvest begins, the God is cut down by the 'death in life' aspect of the Goddess and retreats underground: his spilled blood having regenerated the earth.

At Lammas, Wiccans often bake loaves and make libations of beer to the corn king, the vegetation spirit whose sacrifice ensures the fruitfulness of the land in the coming year. Lammas rituals acknowledge the turn of the season. While witches joyfully celebrate the success of the harvest, they also acknowledge the growing darkness and the lessening power of the sun.

In Ireland the festival is called Lughnasadh (Lugh's mourning). Lugh represents wealth, plenty and the productivity of agricultural land. He is associated with the lightning flash (a fertility symbol) and with thunderstorms, phenomena that commonly occur at the beginning of August.

In Irish mythology Lugh traditionally battles against his grandfather Balor, who embodies the spirit of the wilderness. By conquering Balor, Lugh saves the harvest. He prevents the powers of the wild from destroying agricultural land and returning it to its natural, uncultivated state.

Until very recently many English factories closed for their annual holidays at the beginning of August; a period known as 'Wakes Week'. The workers would spend their free time at 'Wakes Fairs', where it was customary to wear mourning white. Until the nineteenth century, single men and women often forged a partnership for the duration of the fair. Known as 'Telltown marriages' (a corruption of the goddess Tailtu's name) these relationships were accepted as legitimate during the fair. These mirror the Greenwood marriages of Beltane.

Left: The harvest goddess carries the pomegranate and the sickle, symbols of death in the midst of life, of sacrifice at the time of greatest abundance.

JULY 30 – AUGUST 5

July 30

July 31

Lammas.

August 1

August 2

August 3

August 4

August 5

Pale white cakes of barley and oats were once blessed and left on altars as offerings to Hecate at the point where roads crossed.

Triple Goddess Cakes

These oat biscuits can be made in simple rounds to represent the full moon for your esbat gatherings or, for special sabbats, try making Triple Goddess cakes. Once you have rolled out your dough, cut one full moon and two crescent moons for each cake. Using a little milk, attach the two crescent moons. Overlap them slightly on either side of the full moon to create the Triple Goddess symbol.

Mix together 100g (1 cup) self-raising flour, 100g (1 cup) oatmeal or rolled oats, 25g ($^3/_4$ cup) sugar and a large pinch salt. Then rub in 75g ($^1/_2$ cup) salted butter. Add one beaten egg to form a stiff dough. Roll out and cut into full and crescent moons with a round cutter. Bake on non-stick paper for 10 minutes at Gas mark 4, 350 degrees F, 180 degrees C.

AUGUST 6 - 12

August 6

August 7

August 8

August 9

August 10

August 11

August 12

If gathered at midsummer, St John's wort was said to guard the wearer against evil spirits.

Solar Healing Oil

At Lammas, the God has sacrificed himself to protect the harvest. Harness the healing power of the sun to protect you throughout the year. Pack a glass jar with fresh marigold (*calendula officinalis*) petals and top up with organic sunflower oil. Place the jar in a sunny spot and shake it gently every day for about two weeks. Strain the oil into a dark, airtight container and store in a cool place. This oil is excellent for healing cuts, grazes and bites and helps prevent scarring.

Using the same process, you can make an oil with St John's wort (*Hypericum perforatum*). This oil turns a bright scarlet and can be used magically to represent the blood of the God. Applied externally, it speeds the healing of wounds, bruises and sunburn.

AUGUST 13 - 19

August 13

Festival of Artemis, who protects those giving birth, and Hecate, goddess of the underworld.

August 14

August 15

Egyptian festival of Isis, honoured as a goddess of the ripening grain.

August 16

August 17

Norse god Odin sacrifices himself to gain knowledge.

August 18

August 19

*The crown of barley, corn and poppies
symbolizes the fruitfulness of the goddess and*

Encountering the Harvest Goddess

When the fields shine gold with corn and bushes are heavy with fruit, the Goddess shows us her most bountiful aspect. But harvest involves a sacrifice: plants are cut down and seed stored so we can eat, plant and harvest again.

Slow your breathing and still your mind. Find yourself in the middle of a field. It is dark, and the night is mild and still. The scent of the ripe ears of wheat rises warmly around you. The Goddess sits before you on a throne of twisted wood. Her hair is wound through with wheat, oats and poppies and she carries a sickle. Approach her: she may offer you a harvest gift.

When it is time to leave, return to your everyday consciousness. Eat something to ground yourself.

her 'death in life' aspect. It is she who will cut down and sacrifice the Corn King.

AUGUST 20 - 26

August 20

August 21

August 22

August 23

Greek festival of the goddess Nemesis.

August 24

August 25

August 26

Gold is pure, malleable and never tarnishes.
These properties make it an excellent choice in
any magical work.

Crock of Gold Spell

During the waxing moon, line a
cauldron or large bowl with gold
silk or wool. Place in it those
things you associate with wealth.
This could include gold jewellery
and gold coins. Make sure
everything is clean and shining
before it goes into the cauldron.
You could add symbols of the
things you hope to use the money
to achieve, such as a better place
to live, a college course, a holiday
or even a new car.

Burn a gold candle next to the
cauldron for an hour a day until
the moon is full. Every day say:
As the moon grows in the heavens,
so let my wealth grow on earth.
May the God lend his power,
May the Goddess bring it forth.

September

At the beginning of the harvest, at Lammas, the God shed his blood for the land and retreated to the underworld. At the autumn equinox he returns to earth to take the Goddess below ground with him.

After this point, plants stop producing and the land readies itself for the quiet time of winter.

Wiccans celebrate the end of the harvest season at the autumn equinox. Once again they acknowledge the short period when days and nights are of the same length. At this turning point in the year, Wiccans prepare themselves for the shortening days and long nights of the coming winter. They decorate their altars with one white and one black candle to symbolize the equilibrium of the year.

There are different kinds of harvest to celebrate. Some Wiccans will have tended a garden and will have just picked the last of their summer produce. Others will recall the harvest of practical, spiritual or magical achievements of the last year.

Many Wiccans mark the harvest by creating fertility symbols, such as corn dollies. These decorative corn-stalk figures were originally made to capture the spirit of the harvest as it leapt out of the last sheaf of wheat to be cut down. The dolly (possibly a corruption of the word idol) was carried, in honour, back to the farm, where it was carefully preserved. Each year's dolly was kept in a place of safety until the following year's harvest had sprouted and was beginning to grow.

Far Left: Wiccan altars reflect the abundance of the harvest and, to mark the turn of the year, burn one white and one black candle. *Left:* Marked with a pentacle, the loaf symbolizes the harvest of this year's achievements.

AUGUST 27 - SEPT 2

August 27

August 28

August 29
Egyptian celebration of the goddess Hathor.

August 30

August 31
Feast of Hermes.

September 1

September 2

As the year turns, many Wiccans honour the seasons by preserving their fruits. This

Blackberry Cordial

In September, bramble bushes are heavy with fruit and strung with hundreds of gossamer-fine spiders' webs. Pick as many blackberries as you can. You can keep your homemade fruit cordial for your Beltane celebrations next year.

Pick or buy 3 lbs of blackberries, wash, place in a large bowl and stew gently over a pan of simmering water for two hours. Strain through muslin and add 340g (2 cups) sugar to every (500ml) pint of juice. Warm to dissolve the sugar but do not boil. Pour into sterile bottles, leaving a small gap at the top. Screw lids on very loosely, place bottles on an upturned saucer in a deep pan of water and heat to 180 degrees F, 82 degrees C for 80 minutes. When cool, screw tops on tightly, label and store in a dark place.

priestess (above right) offers a cup of blackberry cordial she made the previous autumn.

SEPTEMBER 3 - 9

September 3

September 4

September 5

September 6

September 7

September 8

September 9

Country folk say you should never pick blackberries after the beginning of October because after that they belong to the fairies.

Equinox Incense

This is a smoky, powerful incense to use at your autumn equinox celebrations.

1 part frankincense resin
2 parts myrrh resin
1 part benzoin powder
$^1/_2$ part poppy seeds
1 part storax
$^1/_4$ part barley
9 drops vetiver oil
9 drops patchouli oil
$^1/_2$ part apple peel
$^1/_2$ part blackberries
1 part wine, honey and olive oil mix

Grind the seeds, grains, peel, myrrh and frankincense to a fine powder in a pestle and mortar. Add the benzoin, storax and essential oils and stir in the wine, honey and oil mix. Burn on charcoal discs in a well-insulated censer.

SEPTEMBER 10 - 16

September 10

September 11

September 12

September 13

September 14

September 15

September 16

*The Cerne Abbas Giant (above right), also known
as 'the rude man', is the largest hill figure in
Britain. The figure has been used for approximately*

John Barleycorn

To honour the slain god of the harvest, it is traditional to make a John Barleycorn loaf for Equinox.

Mix together 700g (5 cups) granary flour and a large pinch of salt. Add a packet of fast-acting dried yeast and 50g ($^1/_2$ cup) butter to 425ml ($^3/_4$ pint) of hot water. Add the water mix to the dry ingredients and knead for ten minutes to form a smooth, elastic dough. You could add rye, nuts or oatmeal to your flour. Model your loaf on a fertility-god figure (the Cerne Abbas Giant is a perfect template). Leave to rise for an hour. Glaze with a beaten egg, then bake at gas mark 2, 200 degrees C, 400 degrees F for 40 minutes.

two thousand years as a focus for fertility magic. Up until the last century, women wanting to conceive were told to sleep overnight on the giant.

SEPTEMBER 17 - 23

September 17

September 18

September 19

September 20

September 21   Autumn Equinox.

September 22   Greek Eleusinian mysteries begin in honour of the goddesses Demeter and Kore.

September 23

Undines, the spirits of the element of water, are found riding the eddies and waves of the stream, in still pools and in the deeps of the ocean.

A Water Meditation

Autumn is traditionally associated
with the element of Water, as the
rains swell the rivers and streams.

Imagine yourself beside a river
that flows down to the western
ocean. Step into the stream; the
water supports you easily. Sink
into the current and allow it to
carry you down to the sea. There
is a rush of waves when the river
joins the surf and then a quiet
calm descends as you float into
the embrace of the Great Mother.

Feel the ocean rock you as a
mother gently rocks her child and
then allow yourself to float back
to shore. Eat something to ground
yourself after your journey.

SEPTEMBER 24 - 30

September 24

September 25

September 26

September 27

September 28

September 29

September 30

The Labyrinth Meditation

First create a labyrinth according to the diagram below. You could simply draw it on paper, or, if you have the opportunity, try laying out a labyrinth on a larger scale. You could use stones, rope or, if you are at the beach, pebbles, seaweed, or shells. If you make your labyrinth large enough you can actually walk the maze to the centre and out again.

As you travel into the centre of the maze, concentrate on the coming end of the year. You may want to leave something at the centre to represent the year that has passed. As you return from the centre prepare yourself for the dark season which is still to come.

October

The Celtic feast of Samhain (pronounced 'Sowen'), which means 'summers' end', took place six lunar months after Beltane and marked the end of summer.

At this point sheep and cattle were herded back to their winter pens. Any livestock that could not be fed and maintained over the winter were slaughtered and eaten. Huge bonfires (or bone-fires) were lit to dispose of the remains and this gave rise to the later Saxon name for November, 'the blood month'. Agriculture and herding were abandoned and hunting was resumed for the winter.

As ancient communities relied once more on hunting, they turned again to Cernunnos, the Horned One. His is a unique role. His horns show him to be both the prey that is hunted and master of the hunt. In his aspect as divine, sacrificial king, the God acts as a guide through the gates of death. By Samhain he dwells in the underworld, united with the crone aspect of the Goddess. Wiccans turn to Cernunnos at Samhain in his role as the comforter of those in mourning. His strength, compassion and tenderness bring consolation.

In Wicca, Samhain is seen as an opportunity to feast with death, to remember those we love who have died, and to take the opportunity for particularly effective divination.

At this time of year the veil between the worlds is at its thinnest and communication with other realms is easier. Many Wiccans try scrying with a crystal ball or black mirror to see into the future. Others cast runes or use tarot cards to gain a better understanding of their current situation.

Far left: A Samhain altar, with a dark mirror and crystal ball for scrying, and a skull to symbolize mortality.

Left: A Wiccan priestess tries to predict her future in the dark mirror.

OCTOBER 1 - 7

October 1

October 2

October 3

October 4

October 5

October 6

October 7

Clary (clear eye) sage is ruled by the moon and is traditionally believed to improve second sight and clairvoyance.

Psychic Tea

If you plan to undertake some form of divination at Samhain, try this herbal infusion before you begin. Rosemary improves the memory and sage, long revered as a sacred plant, enhances intuitive power. Dill clears the mind and aids focus while clary sage promotes clairvoyance.

Boil two cups of water in a pan and to it add one teaspoon each of fresh or dried rosemary, sage leaves, dill weed (or seeds) and clary sage flowers.

Allow the tea to infuse for five minutes, then strain and allow to cool. Sip your potion while you enter a meditative state. This tea is quite bitter and, sadly, does not improve if you add honey to it. Instead, try a pinch of salt, which makes it quite a refreshing drink.

OCTOBER 8 - 14

October 8

October 9

October 10

October 11

October 12

October 13

October 14

In the Scottish highlands, the Crone was personified as the 'Cailleach Bheur', the blue-faced hag of the winter.

Crone Meditation

As the season turns towards Samhain, Wiccans often contact the Crone of wisdom. She is the keeper of mysteries of the underworld and we can learn much about ourselves in her care.

Relax, still your mind and find yourself at the mouth of a deep cave. In front of you sits an ancient woman. Her hair is silver and her skin withered, but her spirit is formidable. Around her neck hang crystals and nuggets of gold. She is dressed in the skin of a bear and at her feet a wolf lies, waiting. This is a place of mystery. The crone calls you to her. Close your eyes and enter the safety of her embrace.

When you are ready, thank the Crone and return to your everyday consciousness. Eat something to ground yourself.

The Cailleach withered crops and covered land in snow until her hibernation at Beltane.

OCTOBER 15 - 21

October 15

October 16

October 17

October 18

October 19

October 20

October 21

Moonstone can be used to induce prophetic dreams. Obsidian will aid in grounding and centring. Bloodstone brings courage and energy.

Dedicating a Crystal

As Samhain grows closer and the veil between the worlds becomes thinner, now is a good time to improve your own psychic ability.

Choose a crystal that you feel is in tune with your aims: amethyst or quartz resonate particularly well with intuitive work. Soak your crystal for at least twelve hours in salt water to cleanse it of any unwanted influences. Place the crystal on your altar and then pass it through incense smoke, candle flame, spring water and salt, saying:

May my inner vision be inspired by air, energized by fire, sensitized by water and made wise by earth.

Meditate in front of your crystal for ten minutes every day between now and your planned divination at Samhain to activate your intuition.

OCTOBER 22 - 28

October 22

October 23

October 24

October 25

October 26

October 27

October 28

Treat sacred sites with respect. If you take candles to light your way, never stick them to walls or allow the flame to mark the stones. Never light fires near

Encountering the Ancestors

If you hope to contact your ancestors at Samhain, as many Wiccans do, you may find chanting a useful way of connecting with their ancient energy.

Allow yourself to sink down, travelling further and further back, into an older, earlier consciousness, then begin humming one long note. This note should contain the five ancient vowel sounds found in almost all languages. Start with 'Ah', then allow the note to change to 'Eh', 'Ee', 'Oh' and 'Ooh'. Chant the vowel call three times and wait for the ancestors to speak.

You may receive a message or a symbol to bring back with you. When you have spent enough time with the ancestral spirits, thank them and return to your everyday consciousness. Eat and drink something to ground yourself.

ancient sites. If you want to leave a gift, pour a libation of water on nearby ground.

November

November, when the earth is still and quiet, is one of the most inward-looking periods of the Wiccan calendar.

Samhain signals the beginning of the darkest part of the year, when the days grow shorter and the year turns towards the longest night at Yule.

At this time the Goddess takes on her Crone aspect. She is the keeper of wisdom and mysteries.

In the bleak period between November and the end of December, Wiccans turn instinctively towards inner pursuits such as study, or the planning of next year's projects. They see themselves filled with the dormant possibilities of the coming year and use this time to consolidate their ideas.

Many Wiccans use this quiet, magical period for introspection and self-examination. One could see this time as one of magical hibernation and rest. Wiccans have gathered their resources for the winter and prepare to meet the coming period of greatest darkness. The spiral of the year has almost curled to its most inward point before it begins to spin out again, with the birth of the new sun god at Yule.

Winter is ruled by the element of earth and one of earth's main qualities is the wisdom that is associated with experience. The disc-shaped pentacle of wood, metal or stone is the magical tool associated with the stillness and inward vision of this time of year.

The pentacle can be seen as the foundation stone of practical magical work. On the altar it rests below the bowl of consecrated water and salt that is used to delineate the magical circle and it acts as a shield against unwanted influences. Earth lends the pentacle its qualities of knowledge, patience and thoroughness.

Far left: A Wiccan priestess embarking on an earth meditation uses her metal pentacle as a point of focus.

Left: In November the earth is still and quiet and most plants are dormant.

OCTOBER 29 - NOV 4

October 29

October 30

October 31   Samhain.

November 1

November 2

November 3

November 4

The apple was the Celtic symbol of the underworld and those who hoped to gain the knowledge of immortality were said to seek the

Divination

Samhain, when the veil between the worlds is thin, is the traditional time for witches to undertake divination, in particular to contact their ancestors. On the night of Samhain itself many Wiccans use crystal balls or dark mirrors for scrying (looking into the past or future).

You can also scry by filling a black bowl or a cauldron with water. Position a candle so that the flame is reflected in the dark surface, then allow your attention to float out into the centre of the flame. Become aware of the timeless, eternal space between the worlds and wait there to see if the ancestral spirits make themselves known to you.

silver bough. Cut an apple in half horizontally to reveal the secret pentacle of the goddess within.

NOVEMBER 5 - 11

November 5

November 6

November 7

November 8

November 9

November 10

November 11

'Cernunnos we call upon thee now,
Breast as white as milk, stag of seven tines,
Lip as red as blood, stag of seven tines,

Encountering the Horned One

Still your mind and slow your breathing. It is midday in the forest and the winter sun hangs low in the sky. You hear a noise, turn and catch a glimpse of a huge stag as it leaps past. Before you reach him, the stag is gone.

Following as fast as you can, you suddenly hear drumming and the sound of feet, beating a rhythm on the forest floor. You enter a clearing and see a circle of dancing men. They are twisting and stamping around a horned figure. He is dressed in the skin of a stag and carries the animal's huge antlers on his head. Approach him and he may share his wisdom with you.

When it is time to leave, return to your everyday consciousness. Eat and drink something to ground yourself.

Eye as black as night, stag of seven tines,
We call thee to us,
To guard us through the turning point of the year.'

NOVEMBER 12 - 18

November 12

November 13

November 14

November 15

November 16

November 17

November 18

By knotted one, the thing's begun,
By knotted two, it cometh true,
By knotted three, so mote it be,

By knotted four, the open door,
By knotted five, the spell's alive,
By knotted six, the spell I fix,

Cord Magic

This ancient method of magic has long been used by both witches and magicians. A series of nine knots are tied in a cord while reciting the traditional chant opposite and the cord is then worn on the body for a set period. This period could be from one full moon to the next, or from one sabbat to the next.

Some forms of cord magic use thin cotton thread and the cord is left in place until it rots away naturally. Reaffirm your magical intent as you tie each knot. Tie the final knot extra tightly to complete the spell.

When the time period for your spell is complete, bury the cord, drop it into running water, or untie the knots once again, releasing your intent as you do so.

By knotted seven, the stars of heaven,
By knotted eight, the stroke of fate,
By knotted nine, the thing is mine!

NOVEMBER 19 - 25

November 19

November 20

November 21

November 22

November 23

November 24

November 25

Every Wiccan altar carries a bowl of salt. In every rite, the salt is added to water to cleanse it.

Waning Moon Banishing Spell

When the moon is waning, her energy can be directed towards work that rids us of negative emotions. Under the light of the waning moon, fill a large bowl with water (a cauldron is ideal if you have one). Concentrate on those feelings that are stopping you from achieving your full potential. These might include fear, a lack of confidence or a sense of stagnation.

Write your feelings, or draw a symbol representing them, onto the surface of the water using a black-handled knife. Then stir in a handful of salt. Carefully pour the salt-water into a running stream, or onto bare earth, saying:

I call on the Great Goddess and I call on the Horned Hunter,

As salt purifies water, so let me be cleansed of these emotions

So mote it be!

The purified water is then used both to consecrate the coven members and to mark out the magic circle.

December

On 21 December, the Winter Solstice, the longest night of the year, marks the death of the old year and the birth of the new.

It is at the solstice that the Goddess gives birth to the new God. His birth is echoed symbolically by the birth of the New Year's sun. The new God is sometimes known as the 'Child of Promise' or the 'Child of Light'. It is his role to bring light and life back to the land, while the Goddess lies dreaming underground, waiting for her rejuvenation in spring.

Wiccans celebrate the solstice as Yule; a word probably derived from *geola* (yoke) in Anglo-Saxon or *hweol*, the Old Norse for wheel. Both are appropriate symbols, as the festival yokes the old and the new years together and the turning of the wheel echoes the turning of the seasonal cycle. Yule has always been marked by feasting, drinking and merry-making. For many early communities, winter was a dangerous time. Most villagers had to survive on dried stores and by hunting. Yule brought an opportunity for one last feast before the long wait until spring.

In the bleakest time of the year, Wiccans fill their homes with branches of holly, ivy and mistletoe, reaffirming the power of life in the midst of death. Holly is a symbol of the God; its evergreen leaves and red berries reminding us of the potency of the God's life-blood. Ivy's five-pointed leaves symbolize the pentacle and its curling tendrils the spiral of the year. It is often associated with the Goddess.

Mistletoe was revered by the Celts, who named it 'the golden bough'. The plant was believed to be particularly sacred as its roots grew not in the ground but in the canopy of a tree. Magically, this placed mistletoe 'between the worlds' and imbued it with great power. The white berries, thought of as the semen of the God, were believed to carry great magical strength.

Left: Priest and priestess circle deosil (clockwise) around the solstice fire, celebrating the return of the sun.

NOVEMBER 26 - DEC 2

November 26

November 27

November 28

Festival of Sophia, Greek goddess of wisdom.

November 29

Feast day of Egyptian goddess Hathor.

November 30

December 1

December 2

Frankincense is an excellent addition to any incense. I[...] the mind and allows the breathing to become deep and[...] preparation for magic or meditation.

Winter Solstice Incense

Make this incense before Yule so that the scent can mature and the power of the incense increase.

3 parts frankincense
1 part dried juniper berries
$^1/_2$ part mistletoe berries
5 drops juniper oil
$^1/_2$ part dried orange peel
9 drops bay oil
$^1/_4$ part whole cloves
$^1/_4$ part star anise
5 drops cinnamon oil
5 drops pine oil
1 part dried apple blossom or peel
1 part myrrh resin
2 parts copal resin
1 part wine, honey and olive oil mix

Grind the dry ingredients to a fine powder, then bind the mixture with the oils and wine, honey and olive oil mix. Burn on charcoal in an insulated censer.

stills
, in

DECEMBER 3 - 9

December 3

December 4

December 5

December 6

December 7

December 8

December 9

Cinnamon is a powerful oil, which resonates with solar energy. Oranges have long been seen as

Yuletide Gifts

Nearly all Wiccans give gifts at Yuletide and hand-made gifts are always appreciated at Yule rites.

Yule Incense

Make the incense on the previous page and present it in a beautifully decorated airtight box.

Yuletide Anointing Oil

Try a mix of frankincense, bay, orange, pine and cinnamon essential oils in a base of sweet almond or sunflower oil.

Chocolate Truffle Yule Logs

Heat 75g ($^3/_4$ cup) unsalted butter and 150ml (1 cup) double (heavy) cream to just below boiling point. Remove from the heat and add 250g (10oz) good quality dark chocolate. When slightly cooler, add 2 tbsp brandy or orange juice. Stir as it cools and when almost solid shape into small logs. Dust with icing sugar.

symbolic of the sun because of their colour and shape. Orange oil is sweet, expansive and warming.

DECEMBER 10 - 16

December 10

December 11

December 12

December 13

December 14

December 15

December 16

Solar chant
*'Attis, Mithras, Arthur, Lugh
Baldur, Ra, Apollo, Utu!'*

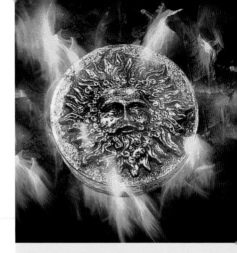

Solar Gods

Yule is a fire festival that celebrates the rebirth of the sun. The theme of the reborn solar god has been celebrated in many cultures since the earliest times. The Roman god Apollo, the Norse god Balder, the Persian god Mithras and the Egyptian god Ra are all archetypes of solar death and rebirth. In ancient Rome the period of solar festivity leading up to the middle of January was known as the *Dies Natalis Invicti Solis* (the Birthday of the Unconquered Sun). There are interesting parallels between the cult of Mithras and, much later, Christianity.

Wiccans can share in the enlightenment of these deities by invoking their energy into the magic circle. Chanting and, even better, drumming are both considered appropriate ways of welcoming solar Gods.

DECEMBER 17 - 23

December 17	Beginning of the Roman festival of Saturnalia in honour of the god Saturn.
December 18	
December 19	
December 20	
December 21	Winter Solstice.
December 22	
December 23	

'The coming year brings a fresh beginning
And like the sun I am renewed and remade.
I leave behind my hurts and troubles,

Greeting the Solstice Dawn

The Winter Solstice is, above all, a time of rebirth and renewal. It is at this point that we should leave behind the old year and look forward to a new beginning. Sometimes it is difficult to forget past hurts or mistakes, both our own and other people's, but carrying guilt or pain around does not do us any good. It is much more useful to try to rectify our own mistakes and to cleanse ourselves of any ill will towards others. We should seek to enhance the useful qualities within ourselves and leave behind those that we no longer need.

Spend the night in meditation and at dawn greet the new sun and the new year. Reaffirm those qualities that you hope to nurture during the next twelve months.

I leave my grievances and my burdens.
For I am a child of the earth and of the infinite heavens,
And my soul is filled with light.'

DECEMBER 24 - 31

December 24

December 25

December 26

December 27

December 28

December 29

December 30

December 31

Mistletoe was particularly revered by the Druids as it lived 'between the worlds', growing with its roots

Mistletoe Good Luck Charm

Mistletoe has always been a symbol of peace, prosperity and fertility. Originally, strangers kissed under the mistletoe to show they had no ill intent towards one another. Mistletoe carries the energizing power of the God, which brings health and happiness.

In folklore, mistletoe was known as 'All Heal' as it was believed to help wounds to heal quickly. Mistletoe is also a plant of protection: it was tied to cradles to protect babies from fairy magic.

To ensure prosperity in the coming year, cut a small sprig of mistletoe from your Yuletide bunch. Make sure it doesn't touch the ground or its power will be lost. Tie it with a decorative red ribbon and suspend it above your front door to provide a blessing of good luck to all who enter.

in the air. Traditionally it was cut with a golden sickle and carried in a white cloth with great ceremony.

Notes

NOTES

NOTES